Contents

(Note: words printed in **bold italics** are explained in the glossary.)

Meet Justine

Do you like being with small children? Justine does. That's why she works as a nursery teacher – and before that, she was a nanny.

The nursery, or kindergarten, where Justine works is a private one. There are four trained teachers: Justine, Lisa (who is the Head), Lesley and Frances. There are also two nursery assistants: Libby and Jo. The pupils are aged between two and five years old. In the mornings, Justine takes an Upper Kindergarten class, that is, the oldest children. In the afternoon she teaches Lower Kindergarten.

▲ Justine doesn't have to wear a uniform, although she sometimes wears a *smock* when the children are painting.

JUST THE JOB!

I work in a Nursery

by Clare Oliver

Photography by Chris Fairclough

FRANKLIN WATTS
LONDON • SYDNEY

First published in 2002 by
Franklin Watts
96 Leonard Street
London
EC2A 4XD

Franklin Watts Australia
56 O'Riordan Street
Alexandria
NSW 2015

ISBN: 0 7496 4057 X
Dewey Decimal Classification 372.21
A CIP catalogue reference for this book is available
from the British Library

Printed in Malaysia

Editor: Kate Banham
Designer: Joelle Wheelwright
Art Direction: Jason Anscomb
Photography: Chris Fairclough
Consultant: Beverley Mathias, REACH
REACH is the National Advice Centre for Children with Reading
Difficulties. REACH can be contacted at California Country Park,
Nine Mile Ride, Finchampstead, Berkshire RG40 4HT. Check out
the website at **reach-reading@demon.co.uk** or email them at
reach@reach-reading.demon.co.uk.

Acknowledgements
The publishers would like to thank Justine Damerell
and the staff, pupils and parents of The Park
Kindergarten, Battersea, London, for their help in the
production of this book.

ustine arrives at 8 a.m. and has an hour to prepare the classroom. Pupils start arriving at 9 a.m. She doesn't really have a proper break until 4.15 p.m. when the afternoon classes go home. Even while Justine is having her lunch she keeps an eye on the children. On Fridays, though, there are no afternoon classes. That means Justine can go home early.

This is the nursery where Justine works. It is one large, bright room. ▶

This is Lisa. She is a 'hands-on' Head, which means that she teaches the children as well as running the nursery and *supervising* her staff. ▲

JUST THE JOB!

Nursery Teacher

Justine's daily tasks include:

- giving the children their lessons
- supervising the children's play-time
- helping to keep the nursery tidy
- planning lessons

Getting Ready

For her first hour at work, Justine is busy preparing everything for the day ahead. When the children arrive, there will be **free play**. Justine and the rest of the team need to set up toys and activities ready for the children.

> Justine snips rolls of old wallpaper into different shapes. Later, the children can use the shapes for collage.

> Justine mixes some powder paint and puts it into the tray of the easel.

Ready for the Day

Here are some tasks that Justine does when she gets in:

- setting up the easels and mixing up powder paint
- stocking the writing table with fresh paper
- putting out jigsaw puzzles and other toys
- tidying the dressing-up clothes
- filling the sand or water tray and choosing toys to go in it

Lisa organises a **rota** to share out the jobs. There are five groups of tasks, one for each member of staff. Each week, Justine's set of tasks changes. The rota is a good system – it means no one gets stuck doing the same job. One important job is filling the washbowls with clean water and stocking up the paper towels. That's because there is no sink in the classroom – but the children get rather messy!

Justine fills the sand tray and selects some toys for the children to play with.

Justine likes the hour she spends before the pupils arrive. It gives her a chance to calm down after the bustle of her journey into work, and get into the right mood for teaching.

The names of the day's *monitors* need to be put up on the board.

Arrival!

The children start arriving at 9 a.m. All of a sudden, the room is filled with noise! Justine or one of the other teachers sits by the door to welcome the pupils. Usually, parents stay at the nursery until their child is settled.

> Justine welcomes the children as they arrive. ▶

For the first 20 minutes after they arrive, the children are free to play. They flit between the different activities that have been laid out. If a child's in the mood to be alone, he or she might draw, do some colouring or sit down with a puzzle. Others may want to be *boisterous* with their friends, splashing about with the toys in the water tray or racing toy cars.

> ◀ Smocks protect the children's clothes. Justine helps the younger children into theirs.

All this time, Justine and the other teachers keep an eye on the children, making sure that no one is left out. They also use this time to chat to the parents.

At the collage table, the children get busy – and sticky!

The children can choose what to play with – and with whom.

Parent Talk

When Justine talks to the parents, she...

- keeps them up-to-date with their child's *progress*
- tells them about any special activities or topics coming up
- *recommends* books for the children to read at home
- lets them know of any *persistent anti-social* behaviour

Language and Numbers

After free play the children split into two groups – Upper and Lower Kindergarten. They pull chairs into two circles for **registration**. Justine reads out the names from her register and ticks off each child as they answer.

> At registration, the children sit in a circle with Justine and Lisa. ▶

Then it's time for lessons to begin. Nursery lessons seem like fun, but that's because they have been carefully planned. Usually, the activities tie in to the nursery's current topic. A topic is a subject that the children explore for a few weeks. At the moment, the topic is 'Homes'. The children might copy out the names of different homes for their writing practice, and count different homes illustrated on flashcards for their number practice.

J ustine introduces an activity by asking the group lots of questions. That way, she leads the children gently towards a subject, and they grasp the activity more easily. Sometimes, she asks one child to **demonstrate** what to do while the others watch. After a couple of hours they have a break when the children can have a drink and a snack.

All the activities are fun! Sometimes, the children don't even notice that they are learning important skills.

Today, it's Maia's birthday. At break, she wears a special hat and there will be a birthday cake to share.

Tricks of the Trade

Justine uses *props* to help her. For example, a maths lesson might involve adding and taking away from groups of

- plastic teddy bears
- toy bricks
- cotton reels
- beakers
- shoelaces

Playing Outdoors

After their break of biscuits and squash, the children go outdoors to work off some energy. The nursery assistants have already taken out toys. Some children just want to chase each other and run around, but there are lots of activities and games to play, too.

Justine asks all the children to line up by the door before they go outside.

The children love clambering all over the sturdy plastic climbing frame.

The nursery is lucky to have an outdoor space, but the teachers need to be extra-alert when they are outside. Not far from the play area is a busy road. The teachers and assistants spread out, for the best all-round view. Sometimes, the children visit the nearby park. Then, the children form a crocodile. There's a teacher at each end of the column, and the other three staff members walk in-between, alongside the children.

Being outside makes the children very excited. Justine watches in case anyone trips and falls, squabbles or sulks. Such young children become upset with each other easily – but they quickly make friends again, too! Justine smoothes the way, encouraging them to apologise and give each other a cuddle.

Justine checks that the games stay friendly and fair.

Justine links up the hopscotch mats and explains how to play. This game helps the children with their counting.

Nursery Assistant

You don't need to be a trained nursery teacher like Justine to work in a nursery. The assistants' jobs include:

- helping to supervise the children when they play
- *escorting* children to the toilets during lessons and breaks
- helping to set up and clear away activities
- letting Lisa or Justine know if they spot a child with a problem

Arts, Crafts and More

After break, there are more lessons. The children are still feeling active, so there is a **creative** project to do. Justine might show the children a new painting technique, such as printing, stencilling or marbling. The children might make papier-mâché sculptures or some simple glove puppets. Whatever the activity, Justine links it in to the current topic.

This morning's activity is cutting out, colouring in and dressing a paper doll.

When the children finish their paintings, Justine will peg them on a 'line' to dry.

On some days, the children have time for a specialist activity after their arts and crafts lesson. They might study French, dance or music. The nursery employs a teacher from outside to give these lessons. It gives Justine and the other teachers time to prepare for story time.

Justine pins up some paintings. Each butterfly will have the artist's name alongside.

Today, Justine is giving a cookery lesson – the children are going to make chocolate birds' nests. Everyone will be allowed to take their nest home, so the assistants make sure each finished one is labelled and placed somewhere safe until the end of the day.

The current topic is 'Homes'. That's why the cookery lesson is making chocolate birds' nests.

Making Birds' Nests

1. Justine puts some blocks of shredded wheat into a mixing bowl.
2. Each child has a turn at crushing the wheat through their fingers – they washed their hands first, of course!
3. The assistants bring up some lukewarm melted chocolate which they have prepared in the kitchen downstairs.
4. Everyone has a turn at stirring the chocolate into the crushed wheat.
5. Justine gives each child a cake case and a dollop of mixture to form into a nest shape.
6. Finally, each child places a couple of small chocolate eggs inside their nest.

Stories and Songs

The children in the morning classes go home at 12.15 p.m. For the last part of the morning, there are some activities to feed their imagination. The teachers tell stories in the story corner, where there are comfy cushions and bean bags for the children to sit on.

> Everyone snuggles up for story time. ▶

Today, Justine is going to tell the children the tale of the 'Three Little Pigs', because it ties in with the 'Homes' topic. The children already know the story, but that doesn't spoil their enjoyment. Everyone joins in to say the Big Bad Wolf's words!

> ◀ Justine tells the story of the Three Little Pigs.

ext to the story corner is the dressing-up area. If there's time, the children dress up and play in some of the different costumes. The children are suddenly **transformed** into cowboys, ballerinas, knights and monsters! Make-believe is a very important part of the children's education.

Finally, the children pull up a circle of chairs ready for some singing. Some songs have actions for the children to do. Sometimes, the children also play musical instruments. Lisa thinks it's very important for the children to finish on an activity they are all doing together, so making music is perfect.

Justine helps the children to put on their dressing-up clothes.

At the end of the morning there is singing. Everyone keeps time with a percussion instrument.

Bang, Beat and Shake

Justine shares out the musical instruments so that, over the term, everyone gets a chance to play each type. There are:

- **drums**
- **tambourines**
- **cymbals**
- **maracas and rattles**
- **wood blocks**
- **triangles**

Teaching Tots

After lunch, new children arrive. Lesley is Head of the Lower Kindergarten. Because she only works in the morning, Justine is responsible for this group in the afternoon. They work on the same topic as the older children, but the activities are much simpler.

This is Lesley. She runs the Lower Kindergarten.

Activities in the Lower Kindergarten are much simpler.

Because the younger children are not so advanced, they need much more one-to-one *tuition*. An assistant helps to supervise a general activity, to free up Justine so she can give individuals special attention. There are lots of specialist toys that are designed to improve the children's *recognition* skills and *co-ordination*. Rather than *focusing on* letters and numbers, most of the activities develop the children's ability to recognise and sort shapes, colours and textures.

Justine helps Max with his spelling. He chooses an object from a little bag, and then uses the letters to spell out what it is. ▼

Justine plays the stroking game with the little ones. They have to pair tiles of the same texture – blindfolded! ▼

Justine starts off one little girl sorting sizes and then lets her continue with the puzzle on her own. ▶

Pros ...

Justine thinks that being a nursery teacher is the best job in the world! It is fascinating watching how young children develop – and very rewarding. Justine teaches them important skills, such as reading, writing and counting. She also helps the children to explore their creative side, through **structured** play and art classes.

Justine likes the way children accept her for who she is – they don't make judgements like adults do.

Justine likes seeing the children play happily together.

Justine enjoys watching how the children **interact** with each other. Nursery prepares the children for infant school, where they will have to cope with being part of a larger social group. Children new to the nursery may be shy or nervous but, within the **supportive** atmosphere, their confidence builds. They discover how to behave with each other and grow to trust their teachers. They share their secrets and stories with them, and this is most rewarding of all.

Justine also enjoys working as a team with the other teachers and assistants. There is time at the beginning and end of each day to chat about the way the children are progressing – and to swap funny **anecdotes** about the things the children have done and said!

It's great to watch as the children become more confident with their writing.

Justine gets on well with her boss, Lisa.

Top Five

These are the things that Justine loves most about being a nursery teacher:

1. The way the children open up to her and share their confidences

2. Seeing how well the children develop in their *academic* lessons

3. Watching how the children play together

4. Working as part of the team

5. Reading stories

... and Cons

Justine finds it hard to think of things that she doesn't like about her job, but it wouldn't suit everyone. Even though Justine keeps the children under control, they still make a lot of noise! It's exhausting being so alert and patient all day, too, making sure that every child is safe and happy.

Once the children have arrived, Justine has no time to herself until 4.15 p.m. Even if the others are watching the children, she will be busy clearing up. This makes the day very tiring. And working with little children brings Justine into contact with everything from coughs and colds to chicken pox and head lice. Of course, she takes time off if she catches something **contagious**, but she knows that will put the other teachers under even more pressure.

Justine uses a dustpan and brush to clear away any mess.

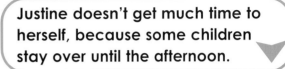

There's lots of tidying up to be done. Libby wipes the messy tables after the cookery class.

Justine doesn't get much time to herself, because some children stay over until the afternoon.

When Justine leaves for the evening, she is often worn out, but it's still not the end of her working day. She might stop off at the library to borrow story books or titles about the current topic. She might read some craft magazines to get ideas for upcoming classes. Or she might have to go and buy equipment or ingredients for the next day's activities.

All of this means extra work for Justine, but she doesn't mind. She wouldn't change her job for anything!

Every spare moment is used to complete some small task that will help keep the nursery running smoothly.

Finding a Job

The main **qualifications** for being a nursery teacher are that, like Justine, you enjoy being with young children. This means that you must be very patient and firm. You will need to be full of ideas so that you can contribute to planning lessons. Above all, you will need training. Justine qualified as a Montessori nursery teacher, and the kindergarten where she works is a Montessori nursery.

A nursery teacher needs to be able to sort out differences quickly and fairly.

It's rewarding seeing the children tell their parents what they've done and learned that day.

Montessori teaching is named after Dr Maria Montessori, who developed a particular method of educating young children at the beginning of the 20th century. In Montessori teaching, the **emphasis** is on encouraging children to learn for themselves. There are Montessori training centres around the world, but because they are private, you will need to pay tuition fees.

Job Know-How

What qualifications do I need?

An NVQ in nursery teaching or similar (such as a Montessori *diploma*).

What personal qualities do I need?

Good with children, patient, gentle, talented at explaining concepts and ideas, imaginative, understanding, punctual and responsible, fit and healthy, good in a team.

How do I apply?

First, you will need to become a qualified nursery teacher. Then, you can look in the press for job adverts (in the local papers, or in specialist educational supplements and magazines), or approach a local nursery direct. Before you are qualified, you could gain experience as a nursery assistant.

Will there be an interview?

Yes – to see how well you will fit in (the team will probably be small). The head teacher of the nursery will also examine your past record with children: if you are newly-qualified, he or she will check how well you did during your work placements.

Lessons need careful planning. Lisa holds a meeting each week, and everyone contributes their ideas.

Another route to being a nursery teacher is to take an NVQ at a college of higher education. Competition for course places is fierce. You will need good GCSE or A Level results and evidence of how well you work with children. Spending time as a nanny after you leave school, like Justine did, is a good way to gain experience – and find out if you really get on well with little ones. Even baby-sitting for neighbours or your own family will help.

Glossary

Academic	To do with formal education.
Anecdote	A short description of something that happened.
Anti-social	Describes something that bothers or disrupts the group.
Boisterous	Energetic and noisy.
Contagious	Describes a disease that can be passed from one person to another.
Co-ordination	Moving all the parts of one's body smoothly and purposefully.
Creative	Describes making something, and using imagination.
Demonstrate	Show.
Diploma	A higher-education qualification.
Emphasis	Stress, most important factor.
Escorting	Going with, accompanying.
Focus on	Give all one's attention to.
Free play	Time when children can choose which activities they do or games they play.
Interact	Mix socially.
Monitor	Pupil who is responsible for certain duties, such as helping at break-time.
Persistent	Constant, repeating.
Progress	Course of development and improvement.
Props	Items that help to explain or show an idea.
Qualifications	Official requirements for a particular job.
Recognition	Recognising or identifying something.
Recommends	Suggests.
Registration	Roll call at the beginning of the day.
Rota	A plan for sharing out duties, so that everyone takes turns.
Smock	A cross between overalls and an apron, worn to protect clothing.
Structured	With a particular plan or shape.
Supervising	Watching over someone.
Supportive	Describes an atmosphere in which one is encouraged and praised.
Transformed	Changed.
Tuition	Teaching.

Find Out More

This is the nursery where Justine works:

The Park Kindergarten
St Saviour's Church
Battersea Park Road
London SW11

Find out more about further qualifications by visiting the NVQ website:
www.dfee.gov.uk/nvq

Visit these website to find out more about Montessori:
http://www.montessori-ami.org/
http://www.montessori.edu/

There are lots of magazines specially for teachers and other people interested in education, including:
Nursery Education
Literacy Time
Maths & Story Time
Numeracy Time
Find out how to subscribe to these at:
www.scholastic.co.uk

Look out for educational supplements in the national papers – the one in **The Guardian** comes out on Tuesdays.

Consider working as a nanny to gain experience with young children. Visit the International Nanny Association website:
www.nanny.org

In Australia you can check out:
Australian Early Childhood Association
www.aeca.org.au
ABC Early Childhood Training College
www.abcectc.com
In New Zealand, contact local polytechnics for nanny training courses, or local childcare centres.

Also, why don't you…

• Visit your local library and check out the careers section. You could also look for books about childcare as well as education.

• Find out if there is a teacher at your school who is an expert careers advisor.

• Look in your local telephone book to find out the names of nurseries in your area and then contact them to see if they need an assistant.

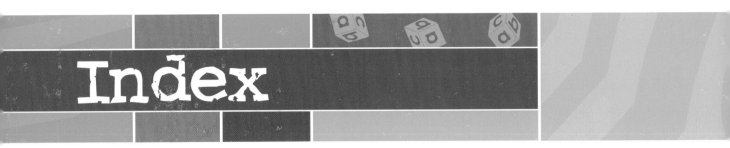

Index